Samuel French Acting Edition

Matt & B~

by Mindy Kah
& Brenda With

SAMUELFRENCH.COM   SAMUELFRENCH.CO.UK

FOR PRODUCTION ENQUIRIES

UNITED STATES AND CANADA
Info@SamuelFrench.com
1-866-598-8449

UNITED KINGDOM AND EUROPE
Plays@SamuelFrench.co.uk
020-7255-4302

Each title is subject to availability from Samuel French, depending upon country of performance. Please be aware that *MATT & BEN* may not be licensed by Samuel French in your territory. Professional and amateur producers should contact the nearest Samuel French office or licensing partner to verify availability.

MUSIC USE NOTE

Licensees are solely responsible for obtaining formal written permission from copyright owners to use copyrighted music in the performance of this play and are strongly cautioned to do so. If no such permission is obtained by the licensee, then the licensee must use only original music that the licensee owns and controls. Licensees are solely responsible and liable for all music clearances and shall indemnify the copyright owners of the play(s) and their licensing agent, Samuel French, against any costs, expenses, losses and liabilities arising from the use of music by licensees. Please contact the appropriate music licensing authority in your territory for the rights to any incidental music.

IMPORTANT BILLING AND CREDIT REQUIREMENTS

If you have obtained performance rights to this title, please refer to your licensing agreement for important billing and credit requirements.

All producers of *MATT & BEN* must give credit to the Author of the Play in all programs distributed in connection with performances of the Play, and in all instances in which the title of the Play appears for the purposes of advertising, publicizing or otherwise exploiting the Play and/or a production. The name of the Author must appear on a separate line on which no other name appears, immediately following the title and must appear in size of type not less than fifty percent of the size of the title type.

(Name of Producer)
Presents
MATT & BEN (100%)
by
Mindy Kaling & Brenda Withers (75%)

In addition, the following credit is required to appear on a separate line on the main credit page in all programs distributed in connection with this piece:

Originally produced Off-Broadway by Victoria Lang &
Pier Paolo Piccoli, Stephen Pevner and Jason Hsiao (50%)

MATT & BEN was originally produced Off-Broadway at P.S. 122 by Victoria Lang & Pier Piccoli, Stephen Pevner and Jason Hsiao. The original set designer was James Youmans, original lighting design was by Jeff Croiter, sound design was by Fitz Patton and costume design was by Anne Sung. The Production Stage Manager was Kelly Varley. The production was directed by David Warren starring Mindy Kaling and Brenda Withers.

CHARACTERS

MATT

BEN

SETTING

Somerville, Massachusetts, 1995.
Ben Affleck's apartment.

BACKGROUND

In 1997, boyhood friends Matt Damon and Ben Affleck won an Oscar for their screenplay *Good Will Hunting*. The success of the film had a remarkable impact on the careers of the young actors, turning Matt & Ben into household names overnight.

Scene 1

(The stage is dark.)

MATT. It's stealing!
BEN. Adaptation is the highest form of flattery!
MATT. Imitation?
BEN. Yes, Imitation. Adaptation. Yes.

(We hear a loud thump.
Lights up: MATT sits on a couch, BEN at a desk. They are staring at a brown paper package lying Center Stage. Together they rise and address the audience.)

BEN. Would you believe a package would fall from the sky?
MATT. From the ceiling!
BEN. Into our laps?
MATT. How does a package fall from the ceiling?
BEN. But it did!
MATT. That's the thing—it did!
BEN. Right in front of us!
MATT. *(Singing)* "A brown paper package tied up with string."
BEN. Amazing things do happen…
MATT. All the time…

BEN. We realize this.

MATT. But not magical things!

BEN. Like a package falling from the sky.

MATT. From the ceiling.

BEN. But it happened to us.

MATT. Interior. Ben's apartment. A lazy Saturday in Somerville, Massachusetts. Stage Right we see a desk, a chair, a computer all untouched. Center Stage we've got a second hand couch. Pan left, we see various junk food and ... Ben. Lights up on Ben, alone at the desk.

(MATT exits.)

(BEN is waiting. He faces the keyboard. He types one letter. Deletes letter. Waits some more. He straightens a pile of paper. Waits some more. Etc. etc. etc. We understand BEN is fidgety and anxious, anticipating Matt's arrival.)

(MATT enters with a pizza. He is out of Ben's line of vision, but BEN senses he is there and begins typing voraciously.)

MATT. Hey Ben.

BEN. Hey, Matt. Long time no see. *Long* time ... *no* see.

MATT. The craziest thing—I'm walking out of Papa Gino's, and I run into Naomi...

BEN. You're like two hours late man.

MATT. No.

BEN. It's twelve thirty!

MATT. Wow. Well, I was just, uh, picking up the pizza-here, I got extra cheese. Anyway, so I ran into Naomi—

BEN. Who is Naomi?

MATT. Naomi from 10th grade, from Ms. Parson's history

class. Naomi! Lesbian. How do I know this? 'Cause she said, 'Hi Matt, how are you, how's the acting doing?" And I said "Can't complain, Naomi. How are you?" and she goes, "Fine. I work in Radio Shack in Arlington, and I'm a lesbian." Just like that. I know! I know! So I was like: "oh Radio Shack? That's cool." And then I left.

BEN. So it took you two hours to get the pizza?

MATT. Yeah, yeah, you know, talked to Naomi, and the drive there, and the drive back, and to find parking there off 128, and parking here... And I... I had to go to this thing first.

BEN. What thing?

MATT. Nothing, just this audition thing.

BEN. Audition for what?

MATT. For nothing. You don't know Shepard? Sam Shepard?

BEN. Yeah, of course.

MATT. Oh, you do?

BEN. Yeah, he was in *The Pelican Brief*, with the wrinkles? I love that guy. Is he in the play?

MATT. Uh, no he wrote the play. It's this play called *Buried Child*. Won a Pulitzer. Anyway, it doesn't matter. It didn't happen.

BEN. What didn't happen? The audition?

MATT. No, I don't know. We'll see.

BEN. What's the part?

MATT. Vince.

BEN. No, what *kind* of part? Is it good?

MATT. Yeah. No Ben, they were looking for a blonde.

BEN. A dark blonde? 'Cause you're not blonde.

(There is a very long pause.)

(Eventually BEN grabs Matt's backpack and begins to rummage through it. He pulls out a script for BURIED CHILD and chucks it huffily on the couch. He plunges back in and produces a beat-up copy of JD Salinger's CATCHER IN THE RYE. He brings the book to the computer and begins to leaf through it.)

MATT. I mean, that's where I was, man.

BEN. I just needed the book so I could go ahead and get started.

MATT. I'm sorry.

(An awkward pause. BEN turns towards keyboard with book. MATT reclines on couch.)

BEN. Are you gonna help?

MATT. Oh, well, you have the book. *(BEN tosses book to MATT—the throw is a little too hard to be friendly.)* Uh, Okay.

BEN. You read and I'll type.

MATT. Yup. I gotta get something to drink …

BEN. No, no, I got it. Here you go.

MATT. Thank you.

BEN. So, I thought we could get through the Stradlater/ Holden scene that starts with page 37. Why don't you read the dialogue—and slowly this time—and I'll just type it in over here. And, as before, please spell any words you think I might have difficulty with.

MATT. *(Reading)* Thirty-seven? Alright, here we go. Holden: "She had a lousy childhood." Lousey is *(BEN begins to type.)* L-O-U-S-no E-Y "childhood. I oughta go down and say hello to her at least." *(BEN continues typing.)* New line. Strad-later: "Why the hell don'tcha then, instead of keep saying it?"

BEN. "Why the hell….?"

MATT. Uh… "don'tcha"—D-O-N-apostrophe-T-C-H-A, "then instead of keep saying it?" *(BEN continues to type.)* I can't believe they give out Oscars for this.

BEN. Give out what?

MATT. Oscars. For adapted screenplay. *(BEN types.)* Are you sure it works this way?

BEN. Uh huh.

MATT. This lifting dialogue just directly from the text—

BEN. Uh huh.

MATT. Why exactly are you sure, Ben?

BEN. What?

MATT. I mean you haven't taken any screenwriting classes or anything, right?

BEN. Wait, is this from the book?

MATT. No. I'm talking.

(BEN loudly deletes the last sentence)

BEN. We do not have time for creative talking.

MATT. If it's really this easy, why do you think this movie has yet to be made?

BEN. 'Cause no one's tried.

MATT. It's a pretty popular book, Ben.

BEN. Well, we haven't tried.

MATT. Doesn't it bother you that the best thing you can produce is just a reproduction of someone else's work?

BEN. That I can produce? And you're just hanging out…

MATT. No, I'm helping out. Doesn't matter. It bothers me a little.

BEN. Why? It's a great story.

MATT. It's someone else's story.

BEN. It's famous!

MATT. C'mon!

BEN. It's public.

MATT. It's stealing.

BEN. Adaptation is the highest form of flattery.

MATT. Imitation?

BEN. Yes, Imitation. Adaptation. Yes. *(To audience)* And that's when it happened.

(MATT reaches behind the couch for package; drops it center where it originally landed.)

MATT. *(Whispering)* We didn't know what it was.

BEN. Or where it came from.

MATT. I was scared.

BEN. Matt was scared. *(He shoots MATT a look.)* Really scared.

MATT. For good reason. But then we realized—

BEN. After we searched the entire apartment—

MATT. That there was no one here and we didn't have to *(MATT gets really loud.)* whisper anymore and we could actually talk in our normal voices.

BEN. BUT JUST TO MAKE SURE THERE WAS NO ONE THERE, WE ACTUALLY TALKED A LOT LOUDER THAN NORMAL. "HEY. WHERE'D THIS COME FROM?"

MATT. I DON'T KNOW BUT IT FELL RIGHT NEXT TO

MY GUN!
    BEN & MATT. The mystery begins.

(MATT and BEN begin to snap in rhythm.)

    BEN. Not ticking.
    MATT. Not a bomb.
    BEN. Not moving.
    MATT. Not an animal.
    BEN. Not three dimensional.
    MATT. Actually, that's three dimensional.
    BEN. No, it's flat.
    MATT. It's flat, but it's three-dimensional.
    BEN. But it's not, like *three-dimensional.*
    BEN & MATT. Where did it come from?
    MATT. We searched the entire apartment. Couch!
    BEN. Fine.
    MATT. Window.
    BEN. Fine.
    MATT. Ceiling?
    BEN. Fine!
    MATT. But it fell from the ceiling.
    BEN. But I'm looking at the ceiling.
    MATT. And?
    BEN. Nothing.
    MATT. Where did it come from?
    BEN. We knew we had to open it. Who would do the honors?

(MATT plunges his hands in his pockets or behind his back.)

MATT. No fucking way.
BEN. So I opened it. *(BEN unwraps the package and reveals a script.)* "*Good Will Hunting.*"
MATT. "By Matt Damon..."
BEN. "And Ben Affleck."
MATT. Is this a joke?
MATT & BEN. We wrote a script.

(Lights down.)

Scene 2

(Lights up. BEN sits on the couch. MATT is at the desk reading the script. Ben is eating some chips loudly. He throws one at MATT.)

MATT. Ow.

(Beat. MATT goes back to reading.)

BEN. Done?
MATT. No.

(Beat.)

BEN. You, like, almost finished?

(BEN throws a chip at MATT.)

MATT. Stop, stop, stop. *(Beat. To audience, in a hush)* This is an excellent script. This is the best script I've ever read. If Ben wrote this, if Ben put this here as joke, then I have severely underestimated his talents.

BEN. Hey, hey check this out! *(During Matt's aside to the audience, BEN has chugged an entire bottle of apple juice.)* One motherfucking sip, huh!?

MATT. *(To audience)* Ok, Ben did not write this. *(To BEN)* I'm done.

BEN. It's so good.

MATT. It's really good.

BEN. It's so good. It's so good, it's so good!

(BEN punches MATT in the stomach playfully.)

MATT. Ben, don't hit me.

BEN. I'm sorry.

MATT. I'm littler than you.

BEN. I know! It's so good!

MATT. *(To audience)* It's kind of, like, too good, man.

(MATT sits on couch and misses BEN picking up and dialing the phone.)

BEN. *(On the phone)* Case! Casey. You will not believe what fucking happened to us!

MATT. Ben!

BEN. We're sitting on the sofa and all of a sudden...

MATT. Ben, hang up.
BEN. What?
MATT. Hang up the phone!
BEN. *(To MATT)* Why?
MATT. Hang up the fucking phone!

(A slight scuffle over the phone)

BEN. OK, OK... Uh, Casey there's this weird thing with call waiting, we might get disconnected, beeeeep. Oh my god, Case, it's happening right now! Yeah, it's weird, I gotta talk to you later. I love you, bye. *(He hangs up.)* What the hell was that about? Why are you locking the door?

MATT. You can't tell everyone, Ben.

BEN. He's my brother.

MATT. This is very confusing. We don't need to involve anyone else yet.

BEN. What's confusing?

MATT. Ben, where do you think this script came from?

BEN. The hand of God. Where do you think?

MATT. I also think God. *(Beat)* Don't you find that strange?

BEN. *(Realizing)* Yes.

MATT. It's amazing.

BEN. It's a blessing.

MATT. It's a gift. *(Pause)* Unless...

BEN. Unless what?

MATT. Have you ever done anything really bad?

(Scary piano music begins to play.)
(Lights down)

Scene 3

(Lights up)

BEN. It's not a curse.

MATT. Why not?

BEN. Because it's not.

MATT. It could be a test. Like Job. Who brags about his family and gets plagued by boils and locusts!

BEN. But what do we have to brag about?

MATT. C'mon, look! We're white, we're American, we're male. We were in *School Ties*! Damn.

BEN. It's definitely not a curse.

MATT. No, not a curse, but maybe a test. Think about it—all that you and I want is what?

BEN. Meatball subs.

MATT. Not right this instant.

BEN. Cable TV.

MATT. More long term.

BEN. Sony Playstation.

MATT. Sony Playstation, no.

BEN. I don't know, money, an Oscar, a girlfriend would be nice, Casey to, like, lose his speech impediment.

MATT. Right! Fame, sex, riches, those are all sins! We're supposed to say no to this. We're supposed to take this script and we get rid of it.

BEN. Uh, absolutely not. I hope you're fucking around.

MATT. Think about this. Why do we deserve this?... We don't. It's a test. Don't you see? It's just like Job.

BEN. We're nothing like Job.

MATT. Not literally, but metaphorically. *(BEN stares at him blankly.)* In terms of, like, a metaphor? *(Another blank look from BEN.)* Okay, a metaphor is a figure of speech you use to compare—

BEN. I know metaphors!

MATT. No, right, but if I were to say "like" or "as" than I'd be using—

BEN. I know what a simile is too. I just don't know what you're talking about—since none of that stuff happened to us!

MATT. I know, that's why it's a metaphor! It's not an exact replica of the situation. It's a comparison—

BEN. Yeah, I know what a metaphor is!

MATT. Apparently not!

BEN. What is your problem?

MATT. My problem is that every time I try to talk about something serious—

BEN. You mean something Lala Land—

MATT. Something serious, you don't even have the vocabulary to discuss it.

BEN. That's not true.

MATT. Yes it is. You dismiss everything—every conversation, every discussion, if it has even slightly complex ramifications.

BEN. Okay, Matt, let's have it your way. Let's have Matt Damon Serious Time *(Spooky voice)* Oh, oh Matt, I'm so scared of this spooky little script. I mean, this is, like, paper bound together with a cover on it. What are gonna do? I mean, what are we going to do?!

MATT. Wow. You're proving my point, man, you're just

proving my point. With every word you're proving my point.

BEN. *(Like a robot)* Proving my point, proving my point, proving my point...

MATT. This is not a joke!

BEN. I know that!

MATT. Really.

BEN. Yes, really. And to be honest, I'm not the one who's screwing around here.

MATT. Oh yeah!

BEN. I mean, what is the point of this conversation? We're not gonna throw it away. I'm not. I'm not gonna let you.... Anyway, Matt, if it's a curse, we're cursed. We can't just, like, put it in the garbage and then just the garbage is cursed. Because the garbage is touching the floor of the apartment ... where we are standing. Yeah, we could throw the garbage out, but it'll just go to some dump, which will be somewhere near us, and like, still on the Planet Earth, where we live. So yeah, maybe if you want to hover above the crust of the Earth in some rocket ship you've invented or something... *(Confused slightly by his own fuzzy logic)* but... *(Dismissing his argument and moving on)* the point is, we can't run away from this, or fly away from this, whatever it is you want to do. Your name is on it, my name is on it, we have to just deal with it!

MATT. I guess.

BEN. And the curse is always wondering about it later if we don't do it.

(MATT is a bit taken aback at Ben's sudden wisdom.)

MATT. That's true.

BEN. Okay?

MATT. Yeah. It's just—

BEN. Matt!

MATT. Then we need to do it right.

BEN. Of course!

MATT. And that's going to be difficult.

BEN. Oh my God!

MATT. We have to get a director.

BEN. Yes.

MATT. And the right location. And the casting—

BEN. Uh huh.

MATT. Plus a crew! I mean, do you know any grips?

BEN. Nope.

MATT. Do we need more than one grip? Grips?

BEN. I don't know.

MATT. Ben, are you even listening to me?

BEN. Yup.

MATT. No, you're not.

BEN. Well, you're just preaching at my face about how to make a movie. I've been in a movie.

MATT. But you haven't made a movie.

BEN. Neither have you!

MATT. Okay, so we both should be concerned here, about getting it just right, because we should both acknowledge this doesn't happen to everyone—

BEN. Okay, I will. I gotcha.

MATT. You will what?

BEN. I will be perfect. I will make a perfect movie with you.

MATT. That's not what I mean.

BEN. Well then, what do you mean? *(There is a pause, and*

it is clear MATT is being evasive about something in particular.)
WHAT!
MATT. You remember senior year—the talent show?
BEN. Yeah, we rocked that fucker.
MATT. Right. *(To audience)* The senior year talent show.

Scene 4

(BEN exits.)

MATT. My first three years at Rindge I entered the talent show with a Shakespearean monologue and won in a walk. Other kids were doing magic, doing impressions, I was doing Shylock and racking up the gift certificates to Applebee's. Senior year could have been no different, but I'm not one to rest on my laurels. I didn't want a trophy, I wanted a challenge, I wanted a change—

BEN. *(Re-entering with a guitar)* He wanted a girlfriend. Suzanne Puglio, 11th grade class secretary and cheerleader, who thought musicians were hot.

MATT. *(Snatching the guitar huffily)* So senior year I learned to play the guitar. And I picked the perfect song to perform. *Bridge Over Troubled Water.* From the Simon & Garfunkel album of the same name. Copyright Columbia Records 1970. Single spent six weeks at number one then goes platinum with more than ten million copies sold. It's dubbed "an anthem of communion" by *Rolling Stone* magazine, it is an exploration of true friendship that speaks to all who hear it.

BEN. "Sail on, Silver Girl"?

MATT. Yeah, it's a bridge, over troubled water, you sail…

BEN. Yeah, you drive on a bridge.

MATT. True, Ben was only a sophomore, but I thought he could handle it. He was popular, he was charismatic, and he'd gotten surprisingly good with the tambourine.

(We hear a loud crash from offstage.)

BEN. Sorry!

MATT. Plus, the whole song is all about friendship, and, you know, Ben was my best friend. So everything seemed to be lining up.

(A lighting change. We are now at the talent show. MATT steps up to an imaginary microphone.)

MATT. Good evening, Rindge and Latin! How's everyone doing out there tonight? *(Silence)* Okay, I'm going to bring you a little tune here tonight, with the help of my good friend, Benjamin Affleck.

(BEN enters the talent show stage, a la his first night at the Oscars, waving to adoring fans, shit-eating grin, tambourine in tow. Various cheers from the "audience" are heard.)

BEN. Guys, shut the fuck up! *(Smiles and winks, encouraging them to cheer.)*

MATT. That's tremendous, thank you.

(In the following section, MATT sings tenderly, sincerely. BEN accompanies inappropriately on tambourine, growing increasingly enthusiastic, eventually resulting in a mockery of the song.)

MATT. *(Singing)* When you're weary…Feeling Small… When Tears are in your eyes….I'll dry them all….
BEN. *(Singing)* O-o-o-ooh la!!
MATT. *(Singing)* I'm on your side…When darkness falls… And pain is all around…Like a Bridge Over Troubled Water….
BEN. *(Overlapping)* Give it up for my best friend in the world, Mathew Damen!! *(Does a Bill Cosby-ish dance)* What is this dance? How do I even know this dance? But somehow I do … really, really well.
MATT. I will lay me down..
BEN. I will lay YOU down, Jenny Warren! I am not kidding. Meet me in the parking lot after the show.

(Laughter erupts. We understand that MATT has lost control of the situation and BEN is now very much center stage. Raucous laughter continues through this next section.)

MATT. What are you doing?
BEN. What?

(Laughter)

MATT. You're ruining it.

BEN. No I'm not.

(More laughter)

MATT. *(To audience)* That isn't even funny!
BEN. Yes it is. *(Laughter)* They think we're a comedy routine, this is way better.
MATT. We won't even get to finish the song.
BEN. So?

(Laughter)

MATT. "Bridge Over Troubled Water" is a classic opus, a composition designed to touch your soul, it takes an audience by surprise—
BEN. It's gay.

(Laughter)

MATT. What?
BEN. It's retarded.

(Laughter)

MATT. Thanks. *(To audience)* Thanks a lot.
BEN. *(Bowing)* Come on, lighten up, we won! We won! *(To audience)* It was fucking awesome and we won. The point is, we did win.
MATT. Fine, so Ben is funny, right? Ben is tall, dark, handsome. Ben is creative. Ben, for instance, uses the made-up word

"chillaxin" because he senses something missing in just "chilling" or "relaxing".

BEN. I mean don't you?

MATT. But Ben is also careless, he's obnoxious, he's oblivious to the point of being dangerous. Ben is the best friend who sleeps with your prom date...

BEN Suzanne Puglio.

MATT. And doesn't even get why you might be pissed about it. He thinks having manners is uptight, he thinks being sensitive is gay—

BEN. I think we won a forty dollar gift certificate and a trophy. And we would've gotten our photo in the school paper, but Noah Barnes-Nessa, the staff photographer for the Rindge Bugle, one time I said something about his sister, Caroline, that she had put on a little weight—she was pretty and everything, I didn't say she was ugly, but she just put on this weight. All right here. It was an observation. But Noah, he hated me, so he ran a picture of the track team that week instead of us. I think Matt was pretty mad about the photo.

MATT. I don't care about the photo.

BEN. It wasn't my fault, it was Noah!

MATT. Obviously it wasn't your fault. It was Noah. But you called his sister fat. So—

BEN. I didn't say fat. I mean I think I just explained it.

MATT. I don't care. It doesn't matter.

BEN. What?

MATT. It wasn't what we planned.

BEN. So?

MATT. So I learned to play the guitar. I practiced for like six weeks.

BEN. Yeah? Well, you didn't have to work that hard.

MATT. I like to work hard.

BEN. For a high school talent show?

MATT. For everything. Look, Ben, you're a funny guy. People like you. You could've burped the alphabet—which I know you can do—and won. But *we* were supposed to do something together.

BEN. We did.

MATT. No. Not the right way.

BEN. Or maybe just not your way.

MATT. Ben, it was a talent show.

BEN. So?

MATT. So, you won for being you, not for being talented.

BEN. So I'm not talented now?

MATT. Well, I guess at making fun of me, yeah, you are.

BEN. I wasn't trying to make fun of you.

MATT. You weren't trying to do anything. Ben, you can't just coast like this forever. It won't get you anywhere.

BEN. Got us first place.

MATT. It wouldn't get you anywhere serious, it wouldn't get you a job, it wouldn't get you into Harvard.

BEN. I didn't want to go to Harvard.

MATT. Fine.

BEN. Not everybody wants to go to Harvard.

MATT. Not everybody can get into Harvard.

BEN. Thanks.

MATT. Sorry, but I mean you just couldn't get in.

BEN. No, no, thank you. I understand.

MATT. But it's because you don't work hard. You don't try and improve. You can't just get better at things naturally, you

have to practice—
    BEN. *(To audience)* There you go.
    MATT. I practice things every day.
    BEN. Ladies and gentlemen, you are about to witness...
    MATT. And practice makes perfect.
    BEN. Classic Matthew Damon.
    MATT. Practice! Practice! Practice!

Scene 5

    BEN. When I first met Matt, it was in drama class at Rindge. we were assigned to do a scene from Samuel Beckett's *Waiting for Godot*. I was so stoked, because no one rehearsed scenes back then, but Matt really wanted to. So we decided to meet up after school at the track. When I got there, I was ten minutes early. Matt was running sprints. I mean really, really hard sprints. *(MATT runs across the stage with determination and alarming speed.)* I don't think he was finished but he saw me waiting there in the stands and came over. *(To MATT)* Hi!

(MATT enters. He checks his heart rate.)

    MATT. *(Mutters)* ...17, 18, 19....
    BEN. You were running so hard.
    MATT. Just one second. *(He finishes counting.)* Not really. Did you bring the script?

BEN. Yeah.

MATT. So, you're Estragon. I'm Vladimir. Do you do a French accent?

BEN. Not really. I do impressions mostly. *(BEN begins to do an accurate but obscure impression of Danny DeVito's The Penguin from* Batman Returns*, complete with mimed top hat and cane.)* The Penguin? Danny DeVito? From *Batman 2*?

MATT. No, not impressions. But I think if we could do, like, a French accent, we could make it really good. Does anyone in your family speak French?

BEN. Well, not my mom or my dad. But Casey might have taken it for a year.

MATT. For a year?

BEN. But I bet he's really good.

MATT. Well, ask him. Can you memorize lines?

BEN. But we don't need to. We only have to do a reading.

MATT. You can't make eye contact if you have to keep looking back at the book. So go home and memorize it. In a French accent if you can. If you can't, call me up so I won't either.

BEN. *(Joking)* Yeah, we can't one of us be speaking with a French accent and the other not. *(Laughs)*

MATT. *(Not joking)* Yeah, no, we can't.

BEN. OK, I'll really try to do one.

MATT. Later. *(To audience)* Matt always knew exactly what the teacher wanted. He liked me because I worked hard and followed his directions and brought snacks to every rehearsal. But later, I think he thought I was a pretty good actor too, because we kept pairing up. But he made us rehearse. And he was fierce about little things, like body posture and especially, eye contact.

(BEN and MATT stare at each other. BEN squirms and looks away.)

MATT. Come on!

BEN. I can't. I want to laugh.

MATT. Just look into my eyes.

BEN. No, man. This is so gay.

MATT. Look into my eyes.

BEN. No. It's too funny.

MATT. It's ok, man, turn around. Put your eyes on my eyes. Look into my eyes. Look into my eyes. Look at my eyes. Look into my eyes. *(BEN closes his eyes so as not to burst out laughing. MATT grabs his face.)* Open your eyes. Open your eyes. Open them. Look into my eyes. Look into my eyes. Look into my eyes. My eyes. Look at my eyes. Ben, look into my eyes. *(BEN looks into his eyes. They have a legitimate moment of weird connection and truth.)* Good. *(MATT smiles.)* We have to do the scene like that. *(BEN lets out a deep breath.)* You have to breathe though.

BEN. Yeah, I'll work on that.

MATT. That was good. That was really good.

BEN. *(To audience)* Sometimes we would do that for 30-40 minutes. Look into my eyes. Look into my eyes. It was pretty fucking weird but sometimes it worked. And I have to say, to this day, Matt is the only person I have no trouble looking straight in the eye. *(They share a genuine moment of connection.)* You can have the Gatorade, you know.

MATT. It's your last one, so…

BEN. You can just buy me a Porche when we're famous.

MATT. If I'm gonna buy you a Porche, I gotta kill the chips

too.

    BEN. Be my guest, if you think your fat ass can take it.

    MATT. Wait, do you think my ass is really fat?

    BEN. No, Fat Damen.

    MATT. What did you say?

    BEN. I said, 'No, Matt Damon, I do not think your ass is fat … Damon.'

    MATT. You just did it again. You called me Fat Damon.

    BEN. No, I didn't. But if I did, that's pretty fuckin' funny.

Scene 6

    BEN. Okay.

    MATT. Okay what?

    BEN. I'm ready. Let's work.

    MATT. Really?

    BEN. Yes, let's do this.

    MATT. We're doing this.

    BEN. Oh my God.

    MATT. You know what this means.

    BEN. I do.

    MATT. We're gonna be famous.

    BEN. Totally famous.

    MATT. I'm gonna meet Steven Spielberg!

    BEN. Yeah you are.

MATT. I'm gonna meet Scorsese.

BEN. True dat. I'm gonna meet Daisy Fuentes!

MATT. Daisy Fuentes?

BEN. Yeah, I like Latin women.

MATT. *(Getting back to work)* Okay. Let's see. Do you have to go the bathroom?

BEN. No.

MATT. We're not breaking. So do you have to go to the bathroom?

BEN. *(Thinks a moment)* I should go.

(BEN exits.)

(MATT patiently watches him go, then frantically dives for the phone. He takes out a card from his pocket, dials the number while keeping one eye out for BEN.)

MATT. *(In a hushed tone)* Hi, this is Matt Damon. *(A little louder)* Matt Damon. No, I can't actually speak up, I'm in a—I have a call back this afternoon at 4? Yeah, for Vince. But I don't think I'm gonna be able to get there till—excuse me? I know I need to be there, I want to be there, I'm kicking my self but if I can be seen just a little bit later—huh? Yeah? He did? I got it? No, yes, that's good, that's great, so never mind. I will definitely be there, um, I just may be a little bit. *(BEN re-enters; MATT does not see him.)* Never mind. I'll see you at four. Thank you so much.

(BEN re-enters quietly, surprising MATT, who quickly hangs up the phone. In doing so, he absentmindedly drops the business card, which gets caught between the couch cushions.)

BEN. Who are you going to see at four?

MATT. *(Caught off guard)* My mom. My mother. Why?

BEN. No reason. You want to leave at four?

MATT. Yeah, I have to. It's this thing … for my mom. It's kind of big.

BEN. Bigger than the script falling from the sky?

MATT. Yes, Ben, believe it or not, there is life outside of this apartment alright, and it's hard, and real people have to deal with real ... hard … things, Ben.

BEN. What are you talking about?

MATT. What am I talking about? What are *you* talking about? Take a look at yourself, man. *(BEN stares in confused silence. Starts to respond. Thinks better of it.)* I'm sorry, man, it's just this…*(MATT rummages through mail on the table looking for inspiration of his next lie)* … personal health issue! Of my mom's.

BEN. OH, man, that's rough.

MATT. Well.

BEN. Wait, is there anything I can do?

MATT. No. No.

BEN. Do you wanna just go right now?

MATT. Oh, no, it's okay.

BEN. No, you should really go, family's more important.

MATT. Nah, the script, I mean, I can wait, till 4.

BEN. Matt, you should go see your mom.

MATT. That's ok, man. I am going to go, but, you know, I think she's being a little melodramatic. Let's get back to work, huh?

BEN. If you say so. Okay.

MATT. So, where were we?

BEN. Uh, page 37.

MATT. Great. Here we go. *(Matt grabs* Good Will Hunting *script, begins reading aloud from it.)* Quick cut to Will, walking across Harvard Yard.

BEN. No, no, no—37 in *Catcher.*

(BEN hands MATT the copy of Catcher.*)*

MATT. Wait, you still want to do that?

BEN. Yeah.

MATT. Catcher?

BEN. Yeah, you're right. We need to commit ourselves to finishing what we start.

MATT. Uh, right.

BEN. It's perfect. If we adapt *Catcher* everyone will believe we could have done that. So we'll finish *Catcher* by the end of next week, shop it around, get picked up … wait up … isn't that what you're talking about?

MATT. Uh, sort of. I think I was just talking about an overall change in your attitude—and mostly in relation to— *(indicating GWH)*

BEN. Hey, you know what, let's make up a schedule of all the times we can meet this week. Let's see, today is Saturday…

MATT. Today I have to leave at four.

BEN. Oooh, right,. So you can be back here by what, like four forty-five? Let's say five.

MATT. Ah, Ben…

BEN. Well what, six? Seven?

MATT. I don't know, Ben.

BEN. Hmmm. Maybe I should just come with you and we

can work on it at your place—

MATT. NO! No.

BEN. No, I mean we'll be quiet and everything, I just don't want to lose our momentum, okay?

MATT. Okay....

BEN. 'Cause I think we can get like five or six good hours in on *Catcher* tonight, if we stay focused. Okay, I'm gonna print up what we've got so far—

MATT. OH GOD MY HEAD!!

(MATT falls behind the couch in agony.)

BEN. Matt!

MATT. One of my migraines!

BEN. You get migraines?

MATT. Yes? Remember? Remember? Remember? Remember? Remember? Remem—

BEN. Yes. Yes, okay? What do you need?

MATT. What have you got?

(BEN rushes offstage to check his medicine cabinet.)
(MATT pops up from behind the couch. He is clearly not in real pain.)

BEN. *(From offstage)* Uh, Aspirin, Bayer, Tylenol, Advil, Aleve, Excedrin, Tylenol PM, Bufferin, and Motrin.

MATT, *(Under breath)* What the fuh? *(To BEN)* Did you say Advil?

BEN. Yeah.

MATT. Do you say, uh, Nuprin?

BEN. No. Do they even sell that anymore?
MATT. Yes! Nuprin, c'mon! That is all that I need!

(MATT falls back behind the couch.)
(BEN re-enters.)

BEN. Okay, okay, I'll run out and get you some.
MATT. Yes! Hurry! I'll pay you back later.
BEN. Yeah, don't sweat it.

(BEN runs out the front door.)
(This next section is spoken as MATT readies himself for his first rehearsal, doing various stretches, vocal exercises, etc. All are ridiculous, but MATT takes them very seriously.)

MATT. *(To audience)* That was pretty good, huh? That's just how Julia Roberts did it in *Steel Magnolias.* She had diabetes. No? *(MATT begins to snack absently.)* Oh come on. I had to! Five or six hours on *Catcher*! Today? The day a script falls from the sky into your living room? It's brilliant, it's got a part for you—it's complete … who thinks the smart choice is wasting the day eating junk food, copying down lines from an old book, and committing plagiarism? Ben, okay? Ben clearly would pick that route. But who thinks maybe you focus on the present? Who thinks you go to rehearsal for the really good part you have very recently been offered, and you read the lines that have actually been assigned to you, with permission from the award-winning author. You don't steal. You don't pull some hack job, you don't even depend on some supernatural gift—you take what you've earned, right? That's growing up. That's reality.

(During the last piece of Matt's speech there is a drastic lighting change—there is an eerie glow to the room. BEN enters as Gwyneth Paltrow.)

BEN. Hi!
MATT. Woah, woah! Who are you?
BEN. Oh, that's right. I'm incognito.

(BEN removes his funny glasses.)

MATT. You're the most beautiful woman I've ever seen. Are you an angel?
BEN. No, no, I'm just … Gwyneth Paltrow. Can you keep a secret?
MATT. Ah, sure. What are you doing here?
BEN. Without Brad? He's in Toronto filming *Seven Years in Tibet* so I'm seven years without a boyfriend. *(She winks.)*
MATT. Uh, would you, like something some food?
BEN. Oh no, I never touch the stuff.
MATT. Right, of course. Sooo, Toronto, huh?
BEN. Mmmhm…
MATT. That's, uh, pretty far away from here, huh?
BEN. Yes, it is.
MATT. It's almost like a different country.
BEN. It is different country. Oh, this is never going to happen.
MATT. What?
BEN. Well, you're making a pass at me, right?
MATT. What! Why? So? No.
BEN.Because Brad will kill you. He'll totally kill you,

'cause you're what, like 5' 6? Well Brad is like 5' 7 and a half and he'll totally kill you.

MATT. Okay! Okay! I gotcha. Sorry.

BEN. Awww…

MATT. No, no, it's just par for the course today.

BEN. Why? What happened?

MATT. Oh, well I don't want to burden you.

BEN. Burden me? It wouldn't be a burden me. I mean why would I have come here and asked for an icky burden. Ok, if you're going to be insulting and presumptuous—I'm just gonna go to my yaga class. Bye!

MATT. No! Wait! I'm sorry. It's just that this has been a really weird day.

BEN. It has?

MATT. Yeah.

BEN. You know what? I've had weird days too.

MATT. This situation has come up—

BEN. Uh-huh.

(Gwyneth begins biting her nails.)

MATT. It's pretty complicated..

BEN, Uh-huh

MATT. And my friend is sort of involved—

BEN. Okay if you see me biting my nails, you really need to tell me to stop at once. Okay, go ahead.

MATT. Basically, I've been offered the chance of a lifetime, but I've done nothing to deserve it.

BEN. Oh. Well you should take it.

MATT. Really? You think so?

BEN. You take it. Take it all the way! Let me ask you something. Do you think I'd be where I am if I wasn't Brad Pitt's girlfriend first? Of course I would be. But I might be thirty!

(Gwyneth begins to chow.)

MATT. It's funny, I always thought you were talented
enough to have made it on your own.
BEN. I know that. But I also know that pride doesn't pay. It
doesn't matter how you get in, silly, because if you're good you
can stay. Oh, are you good?
MATT. Yes. But my friend isn't.
BEN. Oh.
MATT. And I think he's, like, a condition of the agreement.
BEN. Well, here's an anecdote that might help you. Hypothetically, I am cast in the movie *The Pallbearer*. David Schwimmer is also cast in this movie. Hypothetically, David Schwimmer
is a TV actor with one expression and he looks like a mushroom.
Do I do the movie? *(Pause)* Well of course I do! I get a lot of
circulation, I become a big star. So you need to do a movie!
MATT. Oh, I've done movies! I was in *School Ties*.

(MATT gestures to a framed poster of School Ties *hanging on the
wall behind him.)*

BEN. Oh, that is not a good movie.
MATT. Oh.
BEN. Here's what you should do. You need to finish that
script, you need to do this movie, you need to make sure you
have a big part, and you need to keep this cupcake away from me,

I am becoming a huge lardass. That's pretty much it. That's the best advice I can give you and— *(She spots Ben's framed head-shot on the coffee table.)* WHO IS THIS? Who is this? Who is this? Who is this gorgeous, gorgeous man?

MATT. Oh, that's Ben. That's the friend I was telling you about. This is his apartment.

BEN. He lives here? Where specifically?

MATT. That's his bedroom.

BEN. Oh, his bedroom. That's very interesting. I'm going to see if he needs any advice. Good luck with your problems!

MATT. Wait! He's not in there. Hello? Miss Paltrow?

(Gwyneth exits to Ben's bedroom. Lights return to normal. BEN re-enters through the apartment door as himself. He carries six economy-size bottles of Nuprin.)

BEN, Hey man. *(He is out of breath from running back from the store.)* How's your head?

MATT. Better.

BEN. Better?

MATT. I had something to eat. I took a nap. An, uh, Gwyneth Paltrow helped me out.

BEN. Oh, yeah … Gwyneth Paltrow helps me out all the time.

(BEN chucks the bottles of Nuprin and settles down at his desk.)

MATT. *(To audience)* Gwyneth was right. Regardless of the fact that I didn't write word one of this script, and that my best friend is sort of an idiot, I had to do *Good Will Hunting*. Good things come in strange packages. Who knows? If it hadn't been for Ben I may never have been in this right place at this right time. Sure. I'll do it. So long as my name comes first.

Scene 7

(Lights up)

MATT. Alright, so big break-up scene, right? Skylar's dorm. Page 76. Here we go.

BEN. Hey, you know what, let's do it on our feet.

MATT. Yeah?

BEN. Let's get the blood moving; see how it feels.

MATT. Okay. Let's say I'll play, uh, Will. You play Skylar.

BEN. Do you want English Skylar or Regular Skylar?

MATT. Uh … English is fine.

BEN. Right, right.

MATT. Okay...

(They read.)

MATT. *(Reads in the appropriate Boston accent)* "Don't tell me about my world. You're the one that's afraid. You just wanna have your little fling with the guy from the other side of town and marry some prick from Stanford that your parents will approve of. Then you'll sit around with the rest of your trust fund babies and talk about how you went slummin' too once."

BEN. *(Reads in a very overdone cockney accent)* "I inherited that money when I was thirteen when my father died."

(Pause.)

MATT. Less cockney I think.
BEN. Was I doing Cockney?
MATT. A little.
BEN. Oh, I'm sorry.
MATT. It's okay. *(Reading again)* "At least you have a mother."

BEN. *(Again, beginning in a cockney accent)* "Fuck you. You think I want this? That money's a burden to me. *(MATT gives BEN a look; BEN changes to a bad Italian accent.)* Every day I wake up and I wish I could give it back. *(Changes to a bad Southern accent)* I'd give everything I have back to spend one more day with my father. But that's life. *(Changes to a bad German accent)* And I deal with it. *(Resumes the original cockney accent)* So don't put that shit on me. You're the one that's afraid."

(Pause.)

MATT. That's like … weird. That's a weird accent.
BEN. But it's English.
MATT. Yeah, no, we're just gonna drop the accent.
BEN. No, no, it's important. I'll try harder.
MATT. It's just a read through, man.

BEN. C'mon go.

MATT. "What the fuck am I afraid of?"

BEN. "You're afraid of me. You're afraid I won't love you back. And guess what? I'm afraid, too. But at least I have the balls to give it a shot. At least I'm honest with you."

(MATT pauses; gives BEN a look. BEN gestures to keep the scene going.)

MATT. "I'm not honest? Is that what this is about? You wanna hear that I don't really have any brothers? That I'm a fucking orphan? Is that what you wanna hear?"

BEN. "Yes, Will."

MATT. "No, you don't wanna hear that."

BEN. "Yes, I do, Will."

MATT. "You don't want to hear that I got cigarettes put out on me when I was a little kid. That this isn't surgery. Will lifts his shirt revealing a six inch scar on his torso.. You don't wanna hear that. Don't tell me you wanna hear that shit."

BEN. "Yes I do Will."

MATT. "What you wanna come in here and save me? Is there a sign on my back? Is that what you wanna do? Do you? Don't bullshit me. Don't you fuckin' bullshit me."

BEN. *(Overlapping)* No! No there isn't! No! "You know what I want to hear? I want to hear that you don't love me. If you tell me that, then I'll leave you alone. I won't ask any questions and I won't be in your life." *(Sobbing)*

MATT. Will looks Skylar dead in the eye. Lowers his hand. "I don't love you."

MATT & BEN. Oh my god!

(They both mildly freak out)

BEN. That is a fucking good scene.

MATT. Yeah?

BEN. Yeah and you read it really well.

MATT. Thanks. That "I don't love you" at the end. Oh man.

BEN. Forget about it. It's so raw. *(Pause)* Can I give it a go?

MATT. Uh, sure.

BEN. Is that okay?

MATT. We have a lot to do Ben, so we should ... no, we can do it right now if you want. Ok. Great. Good. Here we go.

(They read.)

MATT. "You're afraid of me. You're afraid I won't love you back. And guess what? I'm afraid, too. But at least I have the balls to give it a shot. At least I'm honest with you."

BEN. "I'm not honest? Is that what this is about? You wanna hear that I don't really have any brothers? That I! I am a fucking orphan? Is that what you wanna hear?"

MATT. "Yes, Will."

BEN. "No, you don't wanna hear that."

MATT. "Yes, I do, Will."

BEN. "You don't want to hear that I got cigarettes put out on me when I was a little kid. That this isn't surgery. Will lifts his shirt revealing a six inch scar on his torso. You don't wanna hear that. Don't tell me you wanna hear that shit."

MATT. "Yes I do."

BEN. "What you wanna come in here and save me? Is there a sign on my back? Is that what you wanna do? Do you? Don't bullshit me. Don't you fuckin' bullshit me."

MATT. "You know what I want to hear? I want to hear that you don't love me. If you tell me that, then I'll leave you alone. I won't ask any questions and I won't be in your life."

BEN. "I don't love you!"

(BEN throws a chair across the room.)

MATT. Ben!

BEN. What?

MATT. What is wrong with you?

BEN. What?

MATT. You don't throw a chair!

BEN. No, I think Will is really upset.

MATT. Are you kidding me?

BEN. No. It's the first time he's talking about his childhood.

MATT. Fine, but he's not psychotic. Plus, the chair.

BEN. Forget about the chair. The scene is so fucking intense.

MATT. Why would he break a chair in Skylar's dorm room?

BEN. Because he's got a temper.

MATT. What?

BEN. Yeah, he's a fighter. He's scrappy. Like Daniel Day Lewis in … uh … *My Left Foot.*

MATT. The Boxer?

BEN. Yes, The Boxer. He's got that explosive quality. That "He's been there, He's seen the mean streets. He's got a band-aid over the bridge of his nose."

MATT. No, no, absolutely not.

BEN. Why not? It's good. Let's just try it out.

MATT. No.

BEN. What do you mean, "no"? I want to try it out, so we try it out.

MATT. No, I mean that idea is terrible. Will isn't gonna do that, because it's insane. Look, it doesn't go with the whole tone of his character. Will is a smart guy, but he's not cocky about it. He's got turmoil, but that stays beneath the surface. C'mon, he loves her, but he doesn't know how to show it. He doesn't want her to think he's whipped, you know? He doesn't even want to be in love because it makes him seem weak and if there's one thing Will Hunting doesn't wanna do, it's seem weak. He's saying "I don't love you" at the end not because he's not in love with Skylar, but because he's trying to be strong.

BEN. Okay. Well that all makes good sense, so I can just go to hell.

MATT. Ben.

BEN. No, I mean, that makes good sense, so maybe I should just go to hell.

MATT. Forget it, forget it. Why don't we read something else, like the Chuckie dialogue?

BEN. The Chuckie dialogue?

MATT. Yeah, you'd sound great on him. You know, he'd be more likely to throw the chair so let's read. This is exciting.

BEN. Fuck you, man, Chuckie isn't throwing a chair.

MATT. Why not?

BEN. It's dumbass, it sucks, it's suckass, it's sucko—

MATT. No it's not. It's perfect.

BEN. When the fuck is Chuckie gonna throw a chair? He's got, like, ten lines.

MATT. He has more lines than that.

BEN. I'm not playing Will and you're playing Chucky if

that's what you're thinking.

MATT. Ben.

BEN. This is bullshit, man. These are not your decisions to make.

MATT. Well someone has to make them.

BEN. Oh and that someone is you?

MATT. Yes, Ben, it is.

BEN. Why?

MATT. Because I know what the hell I'm talking about.

BEN. Ohhhhh that's right, Matt. You think you're so much goddamn better than everybody.

MATT. Ben, you honestly feel you could play this part?

BEN. I don't know yet.

MATT. Well I do. I can.

BEN. That is not the point, Matt. Both our names are on that script.

MATT. But that part was written for me.

BEN. By who? Gimme a fucking break, man. I appreciate this deep psychological understanding you have developed for Will fucking Hunting over the last what, like, three hours, but you are not the only person involved. This is my goddamn apartment, and that is my name on the script.

MATT. Yeah, right after mine.

BEN. Are you nuts? "It says Matt Damon AND Ben Affleck". "And," not "with Ben Affleck," not "occasionally including" Ben Affleck!

MATT. "And" my name is first on the script. That's Context clues, Ben.

BEN. Are you fucking kidding me? Okay. I can't take you. Look, here, we'll just flip a fucking coin.

MATT. What?
BEN. That's fair, right?
MATT. No.
BEN. You can call it.
MATT. Heads.
BEN. Heads it's you.
MATT. Good.

(BEN flips the coin. The coin flies across the room and lands by Matt's feet. BEN cannot see the outcome; it's heads.)

BEN. Fine.
MATT. Sorry. Okay, I guess we should move forward then. I guess we should move ahead…. You wanna do two out of three?
BEN. No.
MATT. Really, you don't mind?
BEN. *(Imitating MATT)* "Really you don't mind"?
MATT. Oh, come on.
BEN. "Oh, come on."
MATT. Oh, I really sound like that.
BEN. "Oh, I really sound like that."
MATT. You're such a sore loser, Ben.
BEN. "I'm Matt Damon. I get everything I want. Hey Ben - Two out of three? Two out of three? How about two out of three?"
MATT. Wow, Ben, that is a really excellent impersonation of me. You are a good actor.
BEN. "Wow, Ben, that is real—"
MATT. Stop. Stop! Look man, we made a decision. I think we should try to be professional and move on.

BEN. Okay, I just wanna say one more thing about this and this is the absolute last thing I will say about this, promise. Here it is: If that coin had come up tails, you would have made me keep flipping until it came up heads. I'm not gonna do that. But you would've. Because you're that kind of person. And I'm not that kind of person. And that's it. That's the last thing. Let's get started.

(Pause)

MATT. You know what, Ben, we just won't do it at all. *(MATT throws the script out the front door and slams it shut.)* Forget this. We're acting like kids and you're acting like an asshole.

BEN. Oh, and I'm the only one. Okay, sorry. Sorry. Sorry.

MATT. No, I'm not fighting you every step of the way. It's not fuckin worth it.

BEN. What, we're not fighting.

MATT. It's the same thing every time, okay, I think you and I, we just are never gonna get it together-

BEN. We'll work it out.

MATT. No, we won't. Not this time. I'm done.

BEN. Done with what?

MATT. With everything, okay? Look Ben, we're not in high school anymore. And we're not rich and famous. Obviously, somewhere along the line all the plans we made in the cafeteria, they didn't exactly pan out, so maybe we should just grow the hell up and we'll focus on something else.

BEN. Okay, relax, we'll just work on Catcher for a while.

MATT. I gotta go man.

BEN. Where?
MATT. It's almost four. So…

(MATT gets ready to leave.)

BEN. Ok, when are you gonna be back?
MATT. Listen— *(MATT hangs his head. There is an awkward silence. A knock is heard at the door.)* Did you hear that?
BEN. Uh….

(More knocking)

MATT. That. Here that?
BEN. Yeah, I heard that. *(More knocking)* Did you order food or something?
MATT. No. Can you come sit over here next to me?
BEN. No.

(Knocking)

MATT. Go get it.
BEN. We're working right now.
MATT. It could be Casey.
BEN. You hate Casey.
MATT. No I don't, man. Open the door. *(Knocking)* Just go check.

(BEN goes to the door, exits. He re-enters, perplexed.)

BEN. It's the script.

MATT. What?

BEN. I think it's knocking.

MATT. I don't understand. Does it have a little hand or something?

BEN. Shut up.

MATT. Did you read Christine?

BEN. About the car?

MATT. We're gonna die.

BEN. No, no, it doesn't look angry Matt, calm down. There's not, like, a knife or something,. It's just sitting there quietly.

(Knocking)

MATT. I am so fucking out of here.

(MATT runs into the bedroom.)

BEN. That's good, go hide under my bed.

MATT. *(From offstage)* I will.

BEN. Fruit.

MATT. *(From offstage)* You're the fruit!

BEN. Oh, good one! Okay script. You want a piece of Ben Affleck, you got a piece of Ben Affleck.

Scene 8

(BEN answers the door. There, holding the script, is MATT dressed as JD Salinger.)

MATT. Hello.

BEN. JD Salinger?

MATT. I found this in your hallway. It was cluttering up the space. Hmm.

BEN. Oh my god, come in sir. Come in.

MATT. Oh, alright. I was strolling around Cornish town, lost in my thoughts, per usual, when I wanted upon this shabby little apartment complex.

BEN. Please sit down, sir. Are you hungry? Do you want any food?

MATT. Do you have any pudding?

BEN. Yes! Yes! This is amazing, and, uh, Mr. Salinger—

MATT. Let me guess. You read my book when you were fourteen. It changed your life. You felt like it was written specifi-cally for *you.*

BEN. Oh my god, yes! And right now, my friend and I, this sounds crazy, but we're adapting *Catcher in the Rye* into a screenplay.

MATT. Adaptation is the highest from of flattery.

BEN. Wait, that's exactly how I feel! Oh my god, so you wouldn't mind then, just signing over the rights to us?

MATT. Oh no. I never give out rights. Especially for moving pictures. Commercial flattery? Bah! All you need in life is the brisk air of a New England afternoon and a healthy love for

French wine... *(Sees a woman in the front row)* and French women. Hello, you want some?

BEN. Oh, Mr. Salinger. I think you'll find the adaptation we've done is pretty good.

MATT. Listen to me, young man, you seem quite pleasant. You're very robust, and I'd actually like to help you out, but to tell you the truth, I just sold the *Catcher* rights.

BEN. What?

MATT. Yes, to a charming young Chinaman by the name of Woo.

BEN. Who?

MATT. No, Woo. You know, John Woo. You know, *Face/ Off, Broken Arrow*. He is the master of rockin' action flicks, of kung pao surprise. *Guess Woo's Coming to Dinner? Woo's Afraid of Virginia Woolf?* Woo can it be now? No?

BEN. But, but we were supposed to get the rights...

MATT. Yes, I broke my cardinal rule of artistic independence to be included in the canon of rough-'em-up cinema. For what is a cardinal but a chipper red bird with stardust in his eyes?

BEN. Wait a second, you sold John Woo the rights to *Catcher in the Rye?*

MATT. No of course not. *(Prolonged laughter)* I just told you I don't give out rights. I don't even like talking to people. Let me tell you something. I live by myself, I've always lived by myself. You know why? I don't like pests. I don't like mice, I don't like men, and I don't like John Steinbeck. So I stay far away from all three of them, and I'll advise you to do the same.

BEN. Okay.

MATT. You never collaborate. Collaboration is another

word for compromise. And compromise invariably means the death of creativity. We're born alone, we live alone, and we die alone whether we choose to believe it or not. Don't let it get you down though. Did you really think you'd get the rights to *Catcher in the Rye*?

BEN. Well, kinda…

MATT. Whose bright idea was that?

BEN. It was both of ours actually.

MATT. Is your friend as foolish as you?

BEN. No, Matt's pretty smart actually.

MATT. Maybe he's smarter than you think. *(Salinger picks up the business card Matt dropped on the couch earlier.)* What's this? George Zimmerman, Artistic Director, Cambridge Rep. *(Turns the card over)* See you at 4pm, Studio B. This isn't mine. Is it yours?

BEN. No.

MATT. Must be your friend's ticket to fame.

BEN. What?

MATT. What?

BEN. What?

MATT. What?

BEN. What?

MATT. What? Enough with the questions I never do interviews. Where are my manners. Thank you ever so for the pudding. In regards to your friend, paths that keep crossing, they lead you in circles. You find your own way.

(MATT exits.)
(BEN gets up and goes towards the phone. He cautiously dials the number on the card.)

BEN. *(Practicing)* Hi, this is Matt Damon. Hi, it's Matt Damon. *(Someone picks up the phone.)* Hi, this is Matt Damon. I need to speak to Mr. Zimmerman, Mr. George Zimmerman? Okay, but earlier today I spoke to Mr. Zimmerman—I spoke to *you*. Oh, right, right. Look, Um so when we were talking, I need to be reminded what was said. Yeah, yeah, what you said to me. I remember what I said to you, I said it. Okay. I'm supposed to come in at 4'oclock to audition for the play ... I'm *in* the play? I'm in the play, yeah, no good for me. That's tops. Thank you very much. *(BEN starts to hang up, then decides to add one more comment.)* Oh, also, I might be a little late cause I'm, like, late to a lot of things, you should get used to that. Oh, another thing— I'm not a real blonde like I said on my audition sheet. No, I'm a big, fat lair. Okay, thanks bye.

Scene 9

(A moment later, MATT re-enters as himself.)

MATT. Is it safe? You brought it back in? Are you crazy?

BEN. It's nothing. It was just ... some kids screwing around.

MATT. Oh, I don't think so. I didn't see any kids, you saw kids?

BEN. You know what? We shouldn't do *Catcher*.

MATT. What?

BEN. I just don't think we'll get the rights.

MATT. That's probably true.

BEN. Yeah, and the more I think about it the more I think it's really just a big waste of time.

MATT. Huh.

BEN. You think so, too, right? *(BEN asks this question of MATT a little too pointedly. MATT hesitates in responding. BEN laughs to ease the tension.)* Dumb idea?

MATT. *(Laughing as well, relieved)* I guess so, yeah.

BEN. Yeah, you know what, we're not even writers. We're actors. We should be acting.

MATT. Uh huh.

BEN. Oh man! How did we get so carried away with this? God,! Think of all the auditions we missed.... Or at least I did. *(Beat).* Oh, hey, it's almost four. *(MATT checks his watch. No longer jovially)* You should go see your mom.

MATT. Um.

BEN. Make sure to tell her that I hope she feels better.

MATT. Okay. *(MATT starts to exit, then turns around. He appears unsure about whether to come clean or leave.)* Wait…

BEN. What? Not gonna see her?

MATT. Well…

BEN. Why?

MATT. Ben—

BEN. 'Cause she's not sick? At all?

MATT. No, no, no, come on, look…

BEN. You're fucking busted man.

MATT. Wait. Wait, wait, wait.

BEN. *(Cutting him off, tersely)* Don't. It's not even fun. It makes me sick.

MATT. You don't understand, I couldn't...

BEN. Oh, I understand. You lied to me, I set you up and now you're busted.

MATT. Oh God.

BEN. Yeah.

MATT. What was I supposed to say, Ben?

BEN. What the fuck? You act like a normal person. You say, "Hey Ben, guess what, I got a part in a play."

MATT. Yeah right, and you would have said "That's great, buddy," and then you'd get really quiet and mope around and then start to make fun of the play or the part or the director and warn me about everything that could possibly go wrong, but hey, still, congratulations, have a good time doing that stupid play."

BEN. I would have been happy for you.

MATT. You would have been jealous. You are jealous. That's why you're pissed at me.

BEN. I am pissed at you because you told me your mom had cancer.

MATT. I didn't say cancer.

BEN. Are you for real?

MATT. Hey, if I wasn't so scared of your reaction—

BEN. Don't try to turn this around, you lied to me. You did the wrong thing, not me.

MATT. Fine, Ben, you win, you win. Congratulations, you found me out.

BEN. Oh man!

MATT. You happy?

BEN. You think I like to go on best friend undercover stake-out patrol? That's not me.

MATT. What are you talking about?

BEN. I'm talking about this.

(BEN throws the business card at MATT.)

MATT. Wait. Did you go through my stuff, man?

BEN. No, you left it on my couch, you moron. *(There is an uncomfortable silence. BEN stalks over to the kitchen area and begins eating food loudly, slamming things.)* You should have just told me.

MATT. I didn't know till like two hours ago.

BEN. Not about the play, that doesn't matter,. You should have just told me you didn't want to work on *Catcher*. Then at least I could've started working on it by myself. I would have been done by now.

MATT. Ben.

BEN. But instead, no, you screw around, you go audition for some stupid Sam Shepard play, and you get me excited about a project you know we'll never finish.

MATT. Ben, you can't do *Catcher*. It's a bad idea.

BEN. Why, because you didn't think of it?

MATT. Hey can you listen to me for a minute, I'm saying this to you as a friend. *Catcher* isn't going anywhere, for so many reasons that we shouldn't even get into right now, but come on, you know you're not a writer. You're not supposed to be a writer, you're supposed to be a movie star, you're like this charismatic, action-hero, hang off the side of buildings type of guy.

BEN. Do you think I'm so stupid that I would actually take that as a compliment?

MATT. Ben, I'm being honest. In this industry you have to play to your strengths.

BEN. Oh please Matt, spare me this bullshit know-it-all crap. You with your four lines in some movie-of-the-week, and your god damn Harvard attitude when you didn't even graduate. And you know what—don't tell me about "the industry" and how I should model my career. 'Cause what the hell have you done? Oh right, nothing. All you've done is waste my fucking time!

MATT. I've wasted time? I've wasted your time?

BEN. Yes.

MATT. I made you sit here in this filthy fucking apartment and read easy words to me from a ninth grade book? That's funny Ben that you would say that I've been wasting your time, because I have felt, for like the last ten years that you have been wasting my time. Yeah it's not funny ha ha, it's funny like I want to fuckin' shoot myself.

BEN. Yeah, well don't touch my fucking phone then. It's just that it might have germs on it, since this is such a filthy shithole of an apartment. So maybe you want to get out. In fact, why don't you just get the fuck out.

(BEN knocks some food out of MATT's hands.)

MATT. Right.

(MATT begins to pack his bag and leave, furiously. He reaches for the script.)

BEN. Just get out.

MATT. I'm not gonna leave this here.

BEN. And you're not gonna take it with you.

MATT. Ben, let me explain something for you. The reason

why I am going to leave this apartment with that script is that
God would strike me dead if I left it in the hands of someone like
you.

BEN. Someone like me? Someone who shows up on time,
someone who gives a damn, someone who people actually like?

MATT. Someone who doesn't have any talent. *(BEN
punches MATT in the face. MATT reels backwards and trips over
the couch. He just barely remains standing. Beat)* What the fuck
man?! Are you fucking crazy?

BEN. My headshot!!!

MATT . Oh yeah? You don't like that so much Ben? How
about this. *(MATT grabs a picture of Casey.)* How about this.
Look at this. Hey Casey, how's it going today? Not so good? Not
so good, Casey?

BEN. That's my brother!

*(BEN lunges over the couch towards MATT. MATT counters
    stage right to avoid him.)*

MATT. You broke my fucking jaw!
BEN. Screw your jaw!

(BEN bends down to pick up the photos.)

MATT. Screw your brother! *(BEN grabs a can of soda, begins shaking it ferociously.)* Ben, c'mon...

*(BEN pops open the can and sprays a stream of soda towards
    MATT. MATT blocks it with the pizza box. MATT throws the
    pizza box at BEN; BEN deftly avoids it.)*

BEN. Nice try, 5'8". *(BEN picks up Matt's wallet and fever-ishly begins stuffing money from it into his own pocket.)* Ooh, look what I found. Look at all this cash. Finders keepers.

MATT. Oh yeah, well look at all this fancy expensive computer equipment.

BEN. Don't touch that. *(MATT picks up Ben's computer.)* Put that down.

MATT. What? Put it down?

BEN. Put it down!

MATT. Put it down? Put it where?

(MATT throws it out the window.)

BEN. Are you fucking insane?

MATT. No, you can buy yourself another computer with all the money you just stole from me, you bully thief!

BEN. Okay, I'll do that. It was seven dollars!

MATT. Ben, Ben, no don't do that. Relax man. *(Grabs BEN)* Alright. The tables have turned, compadre.

(BEN lunges towards MATT and begins chasing him. MATT tries to evade him, using couch cushions, clothing, etc. as obsta-cles for BEN. General melee ensues. Eventually they wind up near the script; MATT makes one last stab at grabbing it, but BEN stops him with a shove. He shoves him again. BEN decks MATT; this time MATT is knocked out cold.)
(BEN surveys the situation, the status of his apartment and his unconscious friend.)

BEN. Fuck.

(BEN picks up the script. He throws it down. He storms out of the apartment.)
(Several moments pass in silence.)
(Time has passed. Clock chimes are heard.)
(MATT awakes with a start.)

MATT. It was seven o'clock when I woke up. *(He scans the apartment for signs of BEN.)* My jaw really hurt. I was hoping for an apology. Ben? (MATT rises.) Be-e-e-n? *(He checks the bedroom.)* Ben? You gotta, I guess Ben went out. *(MATT checks his watch, realizes he has completely missed his rehearsal. Defeated, he picks up the script and reclines on the couch. He begins to read it, then sits up with a start. Paging through the script frantically)* It's blank. Every single page. Oh god, oh god. *(He throws the pages on the ground. He runs to the phone and dials.)* Hi, uh, Mrs. Affleck, this is Matthew. I'm looking for Ben. It's kind of an emergency so … oh, no, I'm in his apartment. Right now, like um, khakis, like a button-down shirt, snea—wait. *(Beat)* Is this … is this Casey? Casey, what the fuck is wrong with you? Put him on the phone! Hey! This is important! Just tell him to call me, alright?

MATT. *(To audience)* I didn't mean to treat him bad, I meant to treat him honestly, you know, as a friend. I'm sorry, I'm sorry. I'm sorry? *(He says this last part to God, as if he might earn a reprieve. He rushes to the script and checks the pages once more. They are still blank.)* Oh come on! I'm supposed to take care of him for the rest of my life? Who takes care of me?

(MATT goes to couch and sits. He is extremely discouraged. He truly feels and looks awful.)

(The phone rings.)
(MATT reaches for it on the first ring, thinks a moment, then re-solves not to pick up the call.)
(Ben's answering machine plays: "Hey, this is Ben. I'm not here right now, but I totally wish I was...," followed by a beep and...)

BEN. Hey, uh, Matt, uh, if you're there … if you're not dead *(Pause)* Look, first off, I'm sorry I hit you and knocked you un-conscious. That's not cool cause you're just so much smaller than me. No! Not smaller, forget it. Anyway, so I've been thinking and, uh, I'd hate to see that script go to waste, you know? And I don't think it's gonna work with both of us doing it—I guess be-cause we're so different. Because you are so talented, man, I mean it. And also this is by far the weirdest day of my whole life-so, basically, I want you to have it. I don't know why or how both of our names wound up on there—it's nothing, you know, it's a joke.

(MATT picks up the phone.)

MATT. Ben, uh, it's me…. Where are you?… Oh *(MATT walks over to the window.)*… Oh, yeah, hi, hi, I see you. *(MATT waves.)*…You should come up, man. Yeah.

(MATT hangs up the phone and begins tidying up the apartment. He does not touch the pages strewn on the floor.)
(BEN enters.)

BEN. Hey.

MATT. Hi. You found your keyboard.

BEN. Yup. Yeah.

MATT. Yeah, what do you know?

BEN. Are you okay?

MATT. Sure, forget it. Where did you go?

BEN. Oh, I went for a walk. *(Pause)* Actually, I keyed your car.

MATT. Oh.

BEN. Yeah, and this lady saw me do it and I didn't want her to call the cops so I, uh, got in your car and pretended like it was my car so it just looked like I'd keyed my own car.

MATT. I gotta tell you something.

BEN. I feel really bad about the car.

MATT. Don't worry about the car.

BEN. Okay.

MATT. Look, you're my best friend.

BEN. I know.

(Pause)

MATT. Okay, so, uh … the script is gone. I woke up and the pages were just blank and it's just … gone. *(Long pause. BEN starts to pick up the papers on the ground.)* I don't know how that happened. I think it's my fault. I think I've been taking you for granted and treating you like crap, so … I guess that's my punishment. I don't understand why it has to affect you … so much …too, but I guess that's part of it. I guess it just does. *(BEN has collated the blank pages and taken them over to the computer. He sits.)* But I will make it up to you and, um, I don't know, yet, how this is going to work out, but you know whatever project you want to work on next, it'll be different.

(Yet another pause.)
(BEN feeds one of the pages into the typewriter.)

BEN. It's cool. *(BEN types a few words on the page. We understand it to be a title page for* Good Will Hunting. *MATT moves in to read the computer screen.)* How'd it start? "Interior, bar."
MATT. Yeah, say "South Boston bar."
BEN. Great!
MATT. Ahh, you forgot the…
BEN. Oh, right.

(Lights down.)
(Voice-over: Matt Damon and Ben Affleck's acceptance speech from the 1998 Oscars ceremony.)
(Blackout!)

PROPERY PLOT

A worn sofa (approximately 7' long x 3' wide), with removable pillows or large accent pillows

A beer keg (approximately 2' high) with a square piece of wood (1' 6" square) to create a side table, or something similar in "frat house" style. This side table functions as an end table on the SR end of the couch. It should relate to the height of the couch arm and the top surface should be large enough to hold the base unit for the phone and the standing frame with Ben's headshot.

A small table, preferably with a drawer (approximately 2' 6" long x 1' foot 5" high). This table functions as Ben's desk. The surface area should be large enough to hold a computer monitor and keyboard. Depending on the sight lines in the venue, the computer monitor may be an obstruction on the desk. Therefore, two milk crates should be provided in the event that the monitor would play better on a lower surface next to the desk.

Computer monitor (circa 1995) to fit on top of the above desk. This monitor is not practical and does not need to work.

A CPU (circa 1995) to be set under or downstage of the desk. The monitor should be able to plug into, or appear to plug into, the CPU. The two keyboards (provided by the Production) also need to be able to plug into, or appear to plug into, the CPU (only one at any time). This CPU is also not practical.

A slim chair with no arms for the desk set SR.

A sturdy chair (no arms) that does not fold up and is able to withstand being tossed during the show.

A counter or tall table or side board/bar or even some sort of frat house item (i.e. a Fossball Table on it's side), approximately 4-6' long x 3' high x 18-29" wide. This set piece is used to create a kitchen area US and SR of the SL Front Door unit. Various junk food props and kitchen type set dressings (i.e. Mr. Coffee Machine) should sit on the top surface, and practical food props will be set US of the unit (on existing shelves or perhaps milk crates), so the actors can retrieve the items as if from shelves and cube fridge, which are out of view of the audience.

2 free-standing door units.*

Blacks hung upstage to create the wall of the apartment and to mask the cross-overs and changes from door to door.

A window or a large rectangle able to be hung off a pipe to represent a window upstage.*

A coffee table made of 2 milk crates with a painted board on top (approx. 3' 7" long x 1' 7" wide) or something similar in size that you would find in a college-age guy's apartment.

A practical mic with mic stand and cable.

Perishable items used on stage during the performance *(note: size matters)*:

16 oz Gatorade bottle lemon/lime flavor
16 oz bottle of Coke
10 oz bottle of apple juice
2 large bags of chips (Ruffles and Doritos)
Large pizza box holding one slice of pizza (one slice per show) but weighted to appear to hold a full pizza inside
Snack size pudding w/ a peel off top i.e.: Swiss Miss (one per show)
Large bakery cupcake with vanilla icing (1 per show, should be approximately 3 inches in diameter. If not available, improvise with a large corn muffin and a can of frosting)

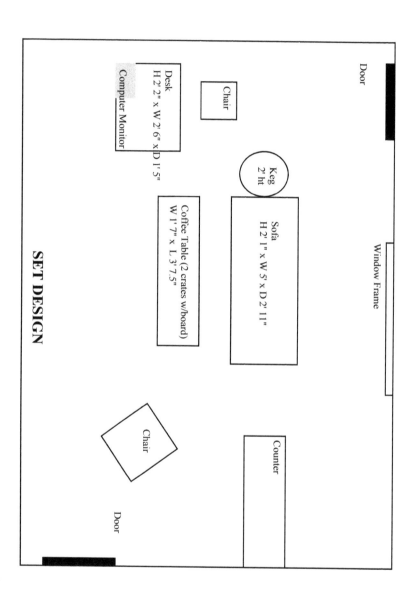

SET DESIGN

Door

Window Frame

Chair

Desk
H 2' 2" x W 2' 6" x D 1' 5"

Computer Monitor

Keg
2' ht

Sofa
H 2' 1" x W 5' x D 2' 11"

Coffee Table (2 crates w/board)
W 1' 7" x L 3' 7.5"

Chair

Counter

Door

Milton Keynes UK
Ingram Content Group UK Ltd.
UKHW051638210324
439914UK00021B/380